CW00673921

FLUTE

All Sorts

GRADES 1–3

Selected and arranged by Paul Harris and Sally Adams

FLUTE PART

Faber Music in association with Trinity College London
Bloomsbury House 74–77 Great Russell Street London WC1B 3DA
fabermusic.com

Contents

© 2002 by Faber Music Ltd and Trinity College London
First published in 2002 by Faber Music Ltd
in association with Trinity College London
Bloomsbury House 74–77 Great Russell Street London WC1B 3DA
Cover illustration by Vikki Liogier
Music processed by Jackie Leigh
Printed in England by Caligraving Ltd
All rights reserved

ISBN10: 0-571-52123-1
EAN13: 978-0-571-52123-4

To buy Faber Music or Trinity publications or to find out about the full range of titles
available please contact your local music retailer or Faber Music sales enquiries:

Faber Music Ltd, Burnt Mill, Elizabeth Way, Harlow CM20 2HX
Tel: +44 (0)1279 82 89 82   Fax: +44 (0)1279 82 89 83
sales@fabermusic.com   fabermusic.com

POLISH DANCE

Demantius was a Bohemian composer who wrote many dances as well
as much church music. This piece was originally for recorder consort.

Christoph Demantius
(1567–1643)

OLD JAPANESE FOLK SONG

The words to this folk song translate as 'Tomorrow is a
shrine visiting day for this baby. What prayer shall I offer up?'

Traditional

MINUET AND TRIO

This very famous Classical composer started composing when
he was five and had written three symphonies before he was ten!

Wolfgang Amadeus Mozart
(1756–1791)

MINUET

This great German Baroque composer taught himself to write music.
He went on to write huge quantities during his long life, including some
important works for flute.

Georg Philipp Telemann
(1681–1767)

THE ELEPHANT *from* CARNIVAL OF THE ANIMALS

'The Elephant' is from Saint-Saëns' *Carnival of the Animals*, one of his most
popular works. Try to imagine an elephant moving when you play this piece!

Camille Saint-Saëns
(1835–1921)

CHILL!

This very relaxed piece should be played in a cool manner, but don't let it drag.
Listening to the swung quavers in the piano part will help you to keep it moving.

James Rae

A TOY

This piece from the late-sixteenth century was written for recorder consort.
'A Toy' was a name often given to more light-hearted pieces.

Anonymous

Allegro vivace ♩ = 100

ƒ (2. **p**)

ƒ (2. **p**)

p (2. **ƒ**)

THE PLOUGH BOY

This English folk song was a favourite tune of Benjamin Britten
(whose *Waltz* appears later in this book).

Traditional

Vivace ♩ = 116

TAMBOURIN

Somis was an Italian violinist and a pupil of Corelli. He went
on to become a composer and formed his own violin school.

Giovanni Battista Somis
(1686–1763)

TYROLEAN DANCE

Krähmer was a Hungarian oboist and composer. He wrote
this piece for a type of Hungarian recorder called a csakan.

Joseph Ernest Krähmer
(1795–1837)

BARCAROLLE

Tchaikovsky is a very famous Russian composer who is best known for
his ballet music and six symphonies. *Barcarolle* was originally for piano.

Pyotr Ilyich Tchaikovsky
(1840–1893)

SWEENEY TODD

Malcolm Arnold is a British composer, also known for his brilliant trumpet playing
in his youth. This piece is from the ballet *Sweeney Todd*.

Malcolm Arnold

HALLELUJAH!

This upbeat piece is a celebration, so play it with lots of confidence and spirit!

Pam Wedgwood

MORESCA

Moresca means Moorish dance. There is no particular style or rhythm associated
with a Moresca, but some think that it developed into the English Morris dance.

Claudio Monteverdi
(1567–1643)

RONDEAU

Naudot was a famous Baroque flautist and composer of many
pieces for his instrument. This was one of his most popular.

Jacques-Christophe Naudot
(1690–1762)

11

ANDANTE *from* CONCERTO IN G MAJOR

Leopold Mozart is best known as the father of Wolfgang Amadeus Mozart!
He was a violinist and composer, and also spent a lot of time training his two
talented children Wolfgang and Anna.

Leopold Mozart
(1719–1787)

CONTEMPLATION

Concone is most famous for his *Songs Without Words*, which are often used
now as exercises for singers. *Contemplation* was originally a piano piece.

Giuseppe Concone
(1801–1861)

WALTZ   No 2 *from* FIVE WALTZES

This famous British composer wrote this piece
when he was only ten years old!

Benjamin Britten
(1913–1976)

Quick, with wit ♩ = 120-144*

* The tempo of the original is ♩ = 176

ROLLER-SKATING

A keen roller-skater, Paul wanted to represent
one of his favourite hobbies in this piece!

Paul Harris

FLUTE

All Sorts

GRADES 1–3

Selected and arranged by Paul Harris and Sally Adams

PIANO SCORE

Faber Music in association with Trinity College London
Bloomsbury House 74–77 Great Russell Street London WC1B 3DA
fabermusic.com

Contents

© 2002 by Faber Music Ltd and Trinity College London
First published in 2002 by Faber Music Ltd
in association with Trinity College London
Bloomsbury House 74–77 Great Russell Street London WC1B 3DA
Cover illustration by Vikki Liogier
Music processed by Jackie Leigh
Printed in England by Caligraving Ltd
All rights reserved

ISBN10: 0-571-52123-1
EAN13: 978-0-571-52123-4

To buy Faber Music or Trinity publications or to find out about the full range of titles
available please contact your local music retailer or Faber Music sales enquiries:

Faber Music Ltd, Burnt Mill, Elizabeth Way, Harlow CM20 2HX
Tel: +44 (0)1279 82 89 82   Fax: +44 (0)1279 82 89 83
sales@fabermusic.com   fabermusic.com

POLISH DANCE

Demantius was a Bohemian composer who wrote many dances as well
as much church music. This piece was originally for recorder consort.

Christoph Demantius
(1567–1643)

3

MINUET AND TRIO

This very famous Classical composer started composing when
he was five and had written three symphonies before he was ten!

Wolfgang Amadeus Mozart
(1756–1791)

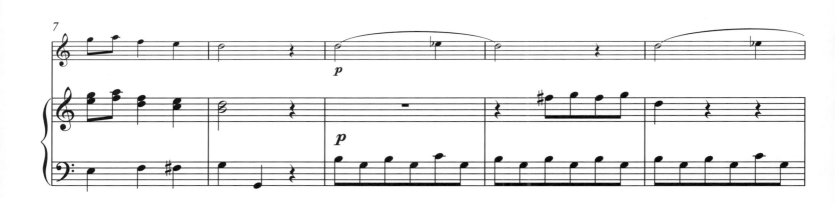

D.C. al Fine

MINUET

This great German Baroque composer taught himself to write music.
He went on to write huge quantities during his long life, including some
important works for flute.

Georg Philipp Telemann
(1681–1767)

THE ELEPHANT *from* CARNIVAL OF THE ANIMALS

'The Elephant' is from Saint-Saëns' *Carnival of the Animals*, one of his most popular works. Try to imagine an elephant moving when you play this piece!

Camille Saint-Saëns
(1835–1921)

CHILL!

This very relaxed piece should be played in a cool manner, but don't let it drag.
Listening to the swung quavers in the piano part will help you to keep it moving.

James Rae

A TOY

This piece from the late-sixteenth century was written for recorder consort.
'A Toy' was a name often given to more light-hearted pieces.

Anonymous

TAMBOURIN

Somis was an Italian violinist and a pupil of Corelli. He went
on to become a composer and formed his own violin school.

Giovanni Battista Somis
(1686–1763)

TYROLEAN DANCE

Krähmer was a Hungarian oboist and composer. He wrote
this piece for a type of Hungarian recorder called a csakan.

Joseph Ernest Krähmer
(1795–1837)

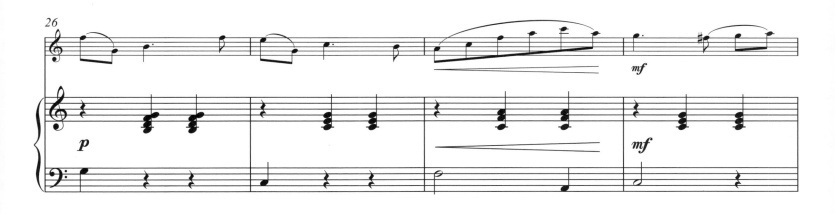
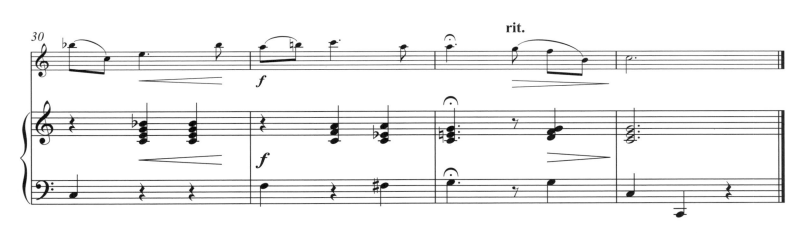

BARCAROLLE

Tchaikovsky is a very famous Russian composer who is best known for
his ballet music and six symphonies. *Barcarolle* was originally for piano.

Pyotr Ilyich Tchaikovsky
(1840–1893)

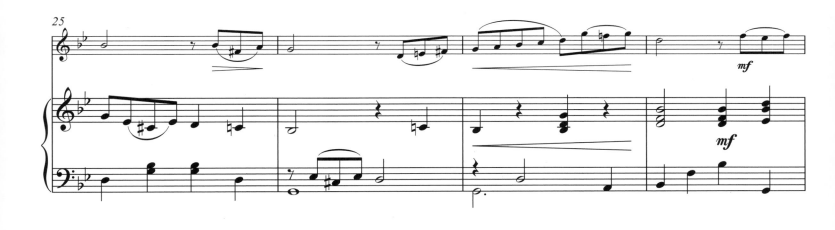

SWEENEY TODD

Malcolm Arnold is a British composer, also known for his brilliant trumpet playing
in his youth. This piece is from the ballet *Sweeney Todd*.

Malcolm Arnold

MORESCA

Moresca means Moorish dance. There is no particular style or rhythm associated
with a Moresca, but some think that it developed into the English Morris dance.

Claudio Monteverdi
(1567–1643)

RONDEAU

Naudot was a famous Baroque flautist and composer of many
pieces for his instrument. This was one of his most popular.

Jacques-Christophe Naudot
(1690–1762)

ANDANTE *from* CONCERTO IN G MAJOR

Leopold Mozart is best known as the father of Wolfgang Amadeus Mozart!
He was a violinist and composer, and also spent a lot of time training his two
talented children Wolfgang and Anna.

Leopold Mozart
(1719–1787)

CONTEMPLATION

Concone is most famous for his *Songs Without Words*, which are often used
now as exercises for singers. *Contemplation* was originally a piano piece.

Giuseppe Concone
(1801–1861)

WALTZ No 2 *from* FIVE WALTZES

This famous British composer wrote this piece
when he was only ten years old!

Benjamin Britten
(1913–1976)

Quick, with wit ♩ = 120-144*

poco Ped.

* The tempo of the original is ♩ = 176

ROLLER-SKATING

A keen roller-skater, Paul wanted to represent
one of his favourite hobbies in this piece!

Paul Harris

UNBEATEN TRACKS

8 contemporary pieces for Flute and Piano

Edited by Philippa Davies

ISBN 0-571-51915-6

Unbeaten Tracks is a ground-breaking new series of specially commissioned pieces for the intermediate player. Combining works by established and up-and-coming composers, this volume brings contemporary music within the reach of the less experienced flautist. The eight pieces (of roughly grade 4 to 7 standard) are written in an array of musical styles, and are an exciting adventure into fresh musical sound worlds.

"I believe this is a wonderful introduction for the flautist to the huge variety of contemporary music out there. The composers have relished the challenge and, while being sensitive to technical limitations, have all written uncompromising musical 'gems'."

Philippa Davies

Carl Davis	*Beatrix*
Daryl Runswick	*Blue Six*
Colin Matthews	*Little Pavane*
Christopher Gunning	*Waltz for Aggie*
David Matthews	*Pieces of Seven*
John Woolrich	*A Sad Song*
Eddie McGuire	*Caprice*
Fraser Trainer	*Outside Lines*